The Happy Moose

By JENNA LAFFIN

Illustrated by BRIAN HARTLEY

Music Produced by ERIK KOSKINEN and
Recorded at REAL PHONIC STUDIOS

CANTATA
LEARNING

WWW.CANTATALEARNING.COM

CANTATA
LEARNING

Published by Cantata Learning
1710 Roe Crest Drive
North Mankato, MN 56003
www.cantatalearning.com

A note to educators and librarians from the publisher: Cantata Learning has provided the following data to assist in book processing and suggested use of Cantata Learning product.

Publisher's Cataloging-in-Publication Data
Prepared by Librarian Consultant: Ann-Marie Begnaud
Library of Congress Control Number: 2015958177
    The Happy Moose
    Series: Me, My Friends, My Community : Songs about Emotions
    By Jenna Laffin
    Illustrated by Brian Hartley
    Summary: A song about feeling happy.
    ISBN: 978-1-63290-551-2 (library binding/CD)
    ISBN: 978-1-63290-577-2 (paperback/CD)
Suggested Dewey and Subject Headings:
    Dewey: E 152.4
    LCSH Subject Headings: Emotions – Juvenile literature. | Weather – Juvenile literature. | Emotions – Songs and music – Texts. | Weather – Songs and music – Texts. | Emotions – Juvenile sound recordings. | Weather – Juvenile sound recordings.
    Sears Subject Headings: Emotions. | Weather. | School songbooks. | Children's songs. | Folk music.
    BISAC Subject Headings: JUVENILE NONFICTION / Social Topics / Emotions & Feelings. | JUVENILE NONFICTION / Music / Songbooks. | JUVENILE NONFICTION / Science & Nature / Earth Sciences / Weather.

Book design and art direction, Tim Palin Creative
Editorial direction, Flat Sole Studio
Music direction, Elizabeth Draper
Music produced by Erik Koskinen and recorded at Real Phonic Studios

Printed in the United States of America in North Mankato, Minnesota.
072016   0335CGF16

ACCESS THE MUSIC!

SCAN CODE WITH MOBILE APP

CANTATALEARNING.COM

We have many **emotions**. We can feel sad, angry, scared, or happy. It is okay to share your feelings with friends and family. We show happiness by smiling and laughing. What makes you happy?

Turn the page to find out what makes Moose and his friends happy. Remember to sing along!

What makes you happy, happy, happy?
I like to be happy, too.

What makes you so happy?
Can you tell me what you do?

Moose is happy
when the sun comes out.

His fur feels nice and warm.
He likes to sing and shout.

Sing and shout,

that's what we do.

Now you can feel happy, too!

What makes you happy, happy, happy?

I like to be happy, too.

What makes you so happy?
Can you tell me what you do?

Robin stays happy
when the sky is gray.

She stays inside her nest,
where she likes to read and play.

Read and play,
that's what we do.
Now you can feel happy, too!

What makes you happy, happy, happy?

I like to be happy, too.

What makes you so happy?
Can you tell me what you do?

Polar bear is happy
when there's snow on the ground.

She jumps, and she **prances**,
and she dances all around.

Dance all around,
that's what we do.
Now you can feel happy, too!

What makes you happy, happy, happy?
I like to be happy, too.

What makes you so happy?
Can you tell me what you do?

What makes you happy, happy, happy?

I like to be happy, too.

What makes you so happy?
Can you tell me what you do?

SONG LYRICS
The Happy Moose

What makes you happy, happy, happy?
I like to be happy, too.
What makes you so happy?
Can you tell me what you do?

Moose is happy
when the sun comes out.
His fur feels nice and warm.
He likes to sing and shout.

Sing and shout,
that's what we do.
Now you can feel happy, too!

What makes you happy, happy, happy?
I like to be happy, too.
What makes you so happy?
Can you tell me what you do?

Robin stays happy
when the sky is gray.
She stays inside her nest,
where she likes to read and play.

Read and play,
that's what we do.
Now you can feel happy, too!

What makes you happy, happy, happy?
I like to be happy, too.
What makes you so happy?
Can you tell me what you do?

Polar bear is happy
when there's snow on the ground.
She jumps, and she prances,
and she dances all around.

Dance all around,
that's what we do.
Now you can feel happy, too!

What makes you happy, happy, happy?
I like to be happy, too.
What makes you so happy?
Can you tell me what you do?

What makes you happy, happy, happy?
I like to be happy, too.
What makes you so happy?
Can you tell me what you do?

The Happy Moose

Americana
Erik Koskinen

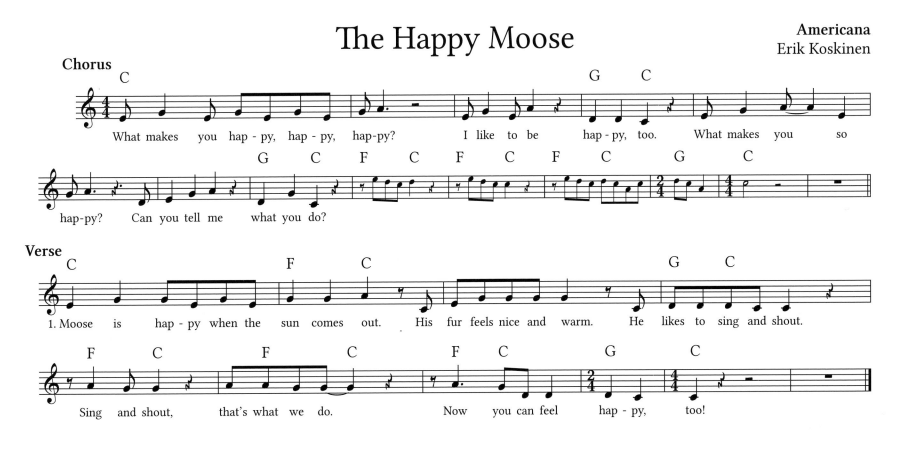

Chorus

What makes you hap-py, hap-py, hap-py? I like to be hap-py, too. What makes you so hap-py? Can you tell me what you do?

Verse

1. Moose is hap-py when the sun comes out. His fur feels nice and warm. He likes to sing and shout. Sing and shout, that's what we do. Now you can feel hap-py, too!

Chorus

Verse 2
Robin stays happy
when the sky is gray.
She stays inside her nest,
where she likes to read and play.
Read and play,
that's what we do.
Now you can feel happy, too!

Chorus

Verse 3
Polar bear is happy
when there's snow on the ground.
She jumps, and she prances,
and she dances all around.
Dance all around,
that's what we do.
Now you can feel happy, too!

Chorus

Interlude

Chorus

23

GLOSSARY

emotions—the feelings that we have, such as feeling happy, sad, scared, or mad

prances–to walk or move in a lively way

GUIDED READING ACTIVITIES

1. Different things make people happy. What makes you happy? What do you do when happy?

2. What makes your mom or dad happy? How about your best friend? What makes your teacher happy?

3. Moose likes the sun, and he sings and shouts when happy. Polar bear likes the snow. She dances and prances when happy. Draw another animal doing something that makes it happy.

TO LEARN MORE

Anderson, Steven. *Happy and You Know It*. Mankato, MN: Cantata Learning, 2016.

Martin, Molly. *Princess Harper Gets Happy*. Minneapolis, MN: Picture Window Books, 2013.

Miller, Connie Cowell. *Happy Is…* Mankato, MN: Capstone Press, 2012.

Thomas, Isabel. *Dealing with Feeling Happy*. Mankato, MN: Heinemann-Raintree, 2013.